GLOSSARY

The Navajo refer to themselves as *Diné*, a word that means "the people." Navajo was a name given to them by Europeans.

acheii (ah-CHA-EE): Navajo word meaning "grandfather."

hágoónee (hah-GOH-nay): There is no Navajo word for goodbye. Instead, they say "Okay" or "All right, then," as in "Okay, things are finished. See you later."

medicine man: A traditional healer and spiritual leader.

mission: A group or organization set up to give help and assistance to people (in this case the St. Bonaventure Indian Mission).

Navajo reservation: A 27,000-square-mile section of land in parts of New Mexico, Utah, and Arizona where the people of the Navajo Nation live.

rez: A nickname for a reservation.

shimá (shih-MAH): Navajo word meaning "my mother."

shimásání (shih-MAH-sahn-EE): Navajo word meaning "my grandmother."

ya'at'eeh (YAH-ah-teh): Navajo greeting, which literally means "It is good" or "It is well."

THE Water Lady

How Darlene Arviso Helps a Thirsty Navajo Nation

BY

Alice B. McGinty

ILLUSTRATIONS BY

Shonto Begay

a·s·b

anne schwartz books

"Thirsty," Cody says, waking up on this cold morning under a starry sky. He reaches for the cup of water near his bed. It's empty.

Though the sun is still asleep over the Navajo Nation,
the kitchen is warm and bustling when Cody walks in.
His mother has just poured water from the bucket near
the sink into a pot for oatmeal.

His grandmother feeds Baby Sister. And Cody's two older
brothers race out the door for school on the reservation.
   Cody climbs onto the counter and looks into the bucket.
Now it's empty, too.

A few miles away, Darlene Arviso
finishes braiding her long, dark hair.

She wakes her grandchildren, helps them dress for school, and makes them breakfast. *Every day, we are blessed,* she thinks as she fills her glass from the sink. She has running water in her trailer. Many families on the reservation do not— no gushing showers, no flushing toilets, no flowing sinks.

As light peeks over the horizon, Cody skips down the wooden porch steps to three big blue water barrels.

He scrambles up and carefully lifts the rock holding one lid in place. He looks inside. Empty. So is the next. And the next.

This is the only water Cody's family has, and it's gone . . . all used up.

What about the animals? Cody checks the chicken coop. No water. He walks down the road to the watering hole where the dogs and horses drink. That's dry, too. He knows that soon, the sun will blaze from the sky, another scorching day in the high desert. And he is *thirsty*.

Once she has dropped her grandchildren at their bus stop, Darlene drives to a parking lot near the Mission school and climbs onto her own bus. As the rising sun floods the rocky land with soft pink light, she begins her route across the rez.

Many miles later, Darlene drops off the students. But her work isn't done. It's time to begin another important job. People are waiting.

After running back home, Cody bursts inside to find his mother. *"Shimá!"* he says, pulling on her skirt. "The water—"

She looks down and whispers, "Shhh! Tell me after I've put the little one down for her nap."

Cody dashes to the sofa. *"Shimásáni,"* he says, pulling his grandmother's arm. "The water! It's all gone."

His grandmother looks up from her quilting. "Don't worry, my child," she soothes. "I know something you do not." And she smiles.

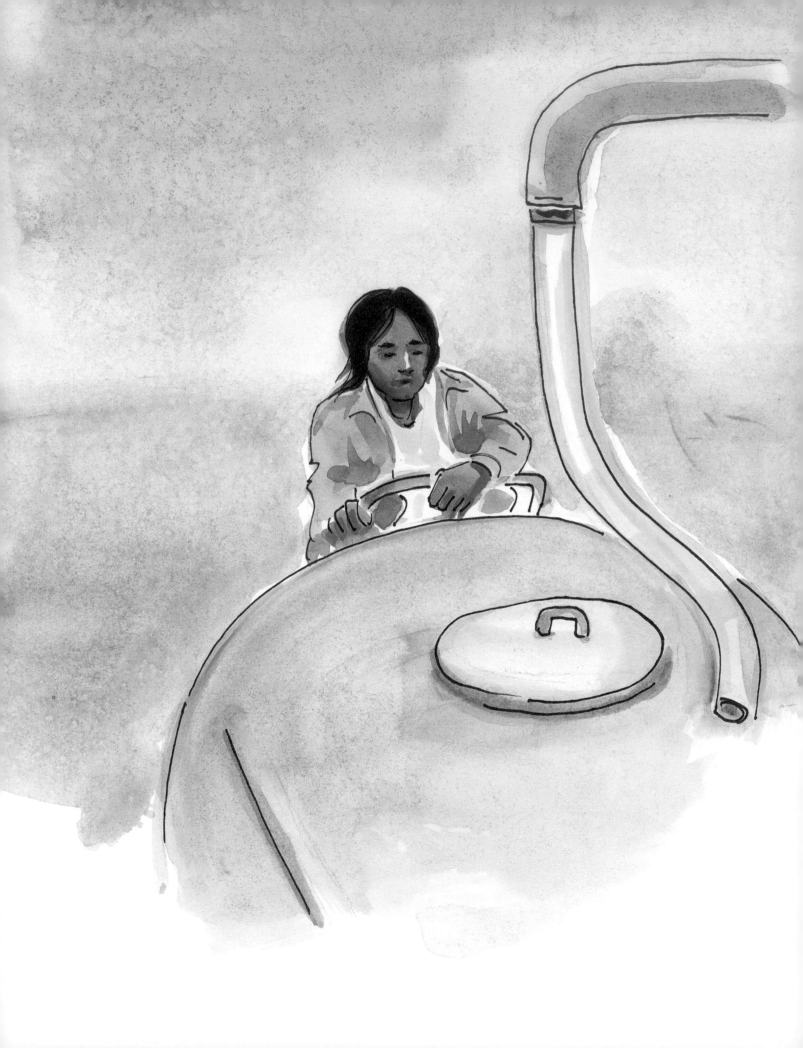

Sunshine gleams on the big yellow tanker truck as Darlene climbs up, up, up its ladder and opens the hatch on top.

Then she reaches for a long pipe attached to the water tower above her and positions it over the hatch. After she flips a switch, water rushes, gushes, through the pipe until the truck's empty belly is full. More than three thousand gallons full!

Now Darlene steps up into the driver's seat and starts the engine. The big yellow truck purrs. She checks her route on the clipboard and steers onto the road.

Cody's grandmother has been telling him a story about the Water Sprinkler, the Navajo God of Water who collects water in a jar and sprinkles it east, west, south, and north to make rain.

When she is done, she takes Cody to the window,
and they look outside.

Thick, dry heat muffles the land as Darlene guides the big yellow truck, heavy with water, up and down steep hills. She winds between mesas and rolls across valleys dotted with sun-baked shrubs.

While she rolls along, waving to other drivers on her way, the Navajo radio station plays softly.

After many miles, Darlene steers the truck onto a ribbon of dirt. At the ribbon's end, a small home sits alone on a windswept hill. Two faces peek through its window.

Cody hears the rumble of heavy wheels, then
sees the big yellow truck. "The Water Lady!" he
cheers. "The Water Lady is here!" He bounds out
of the house.

With a loud "KSSHHhht," the truck comes to a stop. "*Ya'at'eeh*, Cody!" Darlene calls, and she drags the thick hose to the water barrels. She pulls the lever, and Cody watches cool, clean water pour into a barrel.

"Water, water, water!" Cody sings. The chickens cluck. A skinny puppy pads out from under the porch and laps up the drips as Darlene moves the hose to the next barrel.

The sun is beating down by the time Darlene finishes filling all three barrels. Cody dashes inside and a moment later is back with the empty bucket from near the sink. "Don't forget this, Water Lady," he says.

Darlene smiles. "Of course not," she answers, and fills it. Cody carefully takes the bucket from her.

"*Hágoónee,* Cody!" Darlene calls, climbing back into the big yellow truck. She's on her way again.

Darlene will bring water to ten families today and ten more tomorrow. By the end of the month, over two hundred families will have been served. Then she'll start all over.

She knows that the families will make careful use of their gift:

They'll fill the chickens' feeder with just enough fresh water.
They'll catch each drop from a shower to water the flowers.
They'll reuse dishwater to mop floors and bathwater to do laundry.
They'll use laundry water again to wash the car.

While almost every other American will use around a hundred gallons of water today, many on the Navajo reservation will use only seven.

Now Cody's mother helps him place the heavy bucket
back near the sink. At last, he dips his cup into the water.
When he takes a drink and feels the cool water sliding
down his throat, he smiles.

Seventy-five miles later, Darlene bounces the empty-bellied yellow truck back along the road in the sun-soaked afternoon heat. As she drives, she thinks of her *acheii*, her grandfather, a Navajo medicine man who helped his people. She is helping her people, too.

Although she's tired, Darlene climbs back onto the school bus to pick up her students and bring them home.

That evening, as the sun sets over the purple hills of the Navajo Nation, after Darlene has tucked her grandchildren into bed, she washes her face with clean, warm water. Tomorrow, she'll wake up under a starry sky to begin her work again.

Author's Note

The Navajo Nation covers over 27,000 square miles in the states of New Mexico, Arizona, and Utah. It is home to more than 150,000 people. Members of the Navajo Nation elect their own president and vice president and have their own judges and courts. The government is divided into executive, legislative, and judicial branches, and over one hundred local chapters, which make decisions on behalf of their communities.

When I rode with Darlene Arviso (pronounced *ar-VEE-so*) on her water route in March 2016, I was struck by her quiet, open warmth and her devotion to her community. Almost 40 percent of the people living on the Navajo reservation do not have running water in their homes. Darlene delivers 3,500 gallons of water to ten to twelve homes a day, taking a month to visit each of the 220 homes on her route. Sometimes the roads are so muddy, snowy, or frozen that she can't drive on them, so she takes different routes to reach people any way she can.

Though there is much poverty (many Navajo have no electricity), there is a strong sense of community on the reservation. And Darlene is one of the centers of that community. She shares news, lets others know who needs help, and brings people necessities, such as blankets and wood for stoves. She is a friend, psychologist, and social worker as well as the Water Lady. She jokes that the people on her route tell her she can never leave her job.

Darlene knows what it is like to be thirsty in this high-elevation hot desert land, where lips become chapped and dust settles in your nose and throat. She grew up here without running water. As a child, she and her sister would ride horses to the reservoir to drink. Now, though, the reservoir has dried up. There is less rain than before. Much of the water is polluted from nearby mining, making clean, safe water hard to find. For some people, it is fifty miles away.

Many people are working to get water to the Navajo. The St. Bonaventure Indian Mission has a water pump and tower and provides the tanker truck for Darlene's route. In 2017, the mission added a second water delivery truck and driver. Another organization, Dig Deep, is working to dig wells in the area. Wells have to go far into the ground to tap clean water. This is a difficult and expensive project, but Dig Deep is devoted to making it happen.

Hopefully, one day Darlene Arviso will not need to drive the water truck. But for now, the Water Lady will continue to help, with the devotion and caring of a true heroine. "They're all my family now," she says about her people.

SOURCES

Arviso, Darlene, phone interview with Alice McGinty, November 19, 2015.

Arviso, Darlene, interview and ride-along with Alice McGinty, March 21, 2016.

cbsnews.com/news/the-water-lady-a-savior-among-the-navajo

kpbs.org/photos/2015/jan/06/49738

kuow.org/post/many-navajo-nation-water-delivery-comes-monthly

nationswell.com/darlene-arviso-water-delivery-navajo-nation

navajotimes.com/reznews/making-rain/#.VmO5jTZdHug

navajowaterproject.org/stories-2

npr.org/sections/codeswitch/2015/01/06/374584452/for-many-of-navajo-nation-water-delivery-comes-monthly

nytimes.com/slideshow/2015/07/12/us/13water/s/00water-slide-VIWW.html

nytimes.com/2015/07/14/us/on-parched-navajo-reservation-water-lady-brings-liquid-gold.html

uua.org/re/tapestry/multigenerational/gather/workshop1/149426.shtml

windows2universe.org/mythology/tonenili rain.html

A Note from the Water Lady

Every morning that I wake up is a blessing, and every morning I get to share that blessing through my job as the "Water Lady." I help my people by bringing them water, and that brings a smile to my face. I like to see the children come greet me, and to watch their excitement as I fill up their tanks and water barrels. I also get to speak with many different families and elderly people and learn about their days and share stories with them. The biggest joy I get is conversing with everyone along my water delivery routes. Everyone has a different story to tell, and I try my best to help them in any way possible.

My future wishes for my community are that no one will need to haul water to their homes, because they will all have running water. I do hope the younger generation gets more in touch with the elderly and listens to their stories and tales of the old days so that our history and tradition will not be lost.   —Darlene Arviso

For Darlene —A.M.

For all the Water Warriors of the Navajo Nation.
Water Protectors. Toh'ei'iina' (water is life). —S.B.

Text copyright © 2021 by Alice B. McGinty
Jacket art and interior illustrations copyright © 2021 by Shonto Begay

All rights reserved. Published in the United States by Anne Schwartz Books,
an imprint of Random House Children's Books, a division of Penguin Random House LLC, New York.
Originally published by Schwartz & Wade Books, an imprint of Random House Children's Books, a
division of Penguin Random House LLC, New York, in 2021.

Anne Schwartz Books and the colophon are trademarks of Penguin Random House LLC.

Visit us on the Web! rhcbooks.com
Educators and librarians, for a variety of teaching tools, visit us at RHTeachersLibrarians.com

Library of Congress Cataloging-in-Publication Data
Names: McGinty, Alice B., author. Begay, Shonto, illustrator.
Title: The Water Lady: how Darlene Arviso helps a thirsty Navajo nation / by Alice B. McGinty;
illustrated by Shonto Begay.
Description: New York : Schwartz & Wade Books, [2021] | Includes bibliographical references. | Audience:
Ages 4–8. | Audience: Grades K–1. | Summary: Cody is worried when his family on a New Mexico Navajo
reservation runs out of water, but Darlene Arviso, called "The Water Lady," is on the way with her tanker
truck. Includes glossary of Navajo terms and notes about Arviso and life on a reservation.
Identifiers: LCCN 2020011689 | ISBN 978-0-525-64500-9 (hardcover) | ISBN 978-0-525-64501-6 (lib. bdg.) |
ISBN 978-0-525-64502-3 (ebook)
Subjects: LCSH: Arviso, Darlene—Juvenile fiction. CYAC: Arviso, Darlene—Fiction. Water supply—
Fiction. Deserts—Fiction. Navajo Indians—Fiction. Indians of North America—New Mexico—Fiction.
New Mexico—Fiction.
Classification: LCC PZ7.M16777 Wat 2021 | DDC [E]—dc23

The text of this book is set in Lomba Medium.
The illustrations were rendered in watercolor and ink on board.

MANUFACTURED IN CHINA
13 12 11 10 9 8 7 6 5 4